Great

Reviews from Readers

I think the series is wonderful and beneficial for tourists to get information before visiting the city.

-Seckin Zumbul, Izmir Turkey

I am a world traveler who has read many trip guides but this one really made a difference for me. I would call it a heartfelt creation of a local guide expert instead of just a guide.

-Susy, Isla Holbox, Mexico

New to the area like me, this is a must have!

-Joe, Bloomington, USA

This is a good series that gets down to it when looking for things to do at your destination without having to read a novel for just a few ideas.

-Rachel, Monterey, USA

Good information to have to plan my trip to this destination.

-Pennie Farrell, Mexico

Great ideas for a port day.

-Mary Martin USA

Merylee G. Sevilla

Aptly titled, you won't just be a tourist after reading this book. You'll be greater than a tourist!

-Alan Warner, Grand Rapids, USA

Thank you for a fantastic book.

-Don, Philadelphia, USA

Even though I only have three days to spend in San Miguel in an upcoming visit, I will use the author's suggestions to guide some of my time there. An easy read - with chapters named to guide me in directions I want to go.

-Robert Catapano, USA

Great insights from a local perspective! Useful information and a very good value!

-Sarah, USA

This series provides an in-depth experience through the eyes of a local. Reading these series will help you to travel the city in with confidence and it'll make your journey a unique one.

-Andrew Teoh, Ipoh, Malaysia

>TOURIST

GREATER THAN A TOURIST – OTTAWA ONTARIO CANADA

50 Travel Tips from a Local

Merylee G. Sevilla

Merylee G. Sevilla

Greater Than a Tourist- Ottawa Ontario Canada Copyright © 2018 by CZYK Publishing LLC. All Rights Reserved.

All rights reserved. No part of this book may be reproduced in any form or by any electronic or mechanical means including information storage and retrieval systems, without permission in writing from the author. The only exception is by a reviewer, who may quote short excerpts in a review.

Cover designed by: Ivana Stamenković
Cover Image: image provided by the author, Merylee G. Sevilla

Greater Than a Tourist
Visit our website at www.GreaterThanaTourist.com

Lock Haven, PA
All rights reserved.
ISBN: 9781980771128

>TOURIST

50 TRAVEL TIPS FROM A LOCAL

Merylee G. Sevilla

BOOK DESCRIPTION

Are you excited about planning your next trip?

Do you want to try something new?

Would you like some guidance from a local?

If you answered yes to any of these questions, then this Greater Than a Tourist book is for you.

Greater Than a Tourist- Ottawa Ontario Canada by Merylee G. Sevilla offers the inside scoop on Ottawa. Most travel books tell you how to travel like a tourist. Although there is nothing wrong with that, as part of the Greater Than a Tourist series, this book will give you travel tips from someone who has lived at your next travel destination.

In these pages, you will discover advice that will help you throughout your stay. This book will not tell you exact addresses or store hours but instead will give you excitement and knowledge from a local that you may not find in other smaller print travel books.

Travel like a local. Slow down, stay in one place, and get to know the people and the culture. By the time you finish this book, you will be eager and prepared to travel to your next destination.

Merylee G. Sevilla

>TOURIST

TABLE OF CONTENTS

BOOK DESCRIPTION
TABLE OF CONTENTS
DEDICATION
ABOUT THE AUTHOR
HOW TO USE THIS BOOK
FROM THE PUBLISHER
OUR STORY
WELCOME TO
> TOURIST
INTRODUCTION
1. Anthony's Pizza
2. Champlain Lookout
3. Rockcliffe Pavilion
4. Walking Trails Behind Parliament Hill
5. The Manx
6. Lieutenants Pump
7. Pinegrove Trail
8. Watson's Mill
9. A.Y. Jackson Park
10. Aquatopia Conservatory
11. The Brew Pub

Merylee G. Sevilla

12. The Arboretum
13. The Experimental Farm
14. Hog's Back
15. Britannia Beach
16. Petrie Island
17. Planet Coffee
18. Wellington Diner
19. Hip Hop Karaoke
20. House Of Targ
21. Mayfair Theatre
22. Life Of Pie
23. Marble Slab Creamery
24. Westboro Pumpkin Walk
25. Flying Squirrel Trampoline Park
26. Produce Depot
27. Ozzy's Shawarma
28. The Green Door
29. Strathcona Park
30. Path Behind Canadian Museum of History
31. House of Georgie And Sorento's
32. Thyme And Again
33. Funhaven
34. Princess Louise Waterfalls
35. Chelsea Pub
36. The Lookout

37. Bad Axe Throwing
38. Burgers And Shakes
39. Jaymes White Show
40. The Loft
41. Saunders Farm
42. Park Omega
43. The Maze - Maple Hill Urban Farm
44. Karter's Korner
45. Rideau Carleton Horse Racing
46. Elgin Street Diner
47. Ottawa Fury Game
48. Ottawa's Christmas Light Show
49. Stoneface Dolly's
50. Valleyview Farm

TOP REASONS TO BOOK THIS TRIP

50 THINGS TO KNOW ABOUT PACKING LIGHT FOR TRAVEL

\> TOURIST

GREATER THAN A TOURIST

\> TOURIST

GREATER THAN A TOURIST

NOTES

Merylee G. Sevilla

DEDICATION

This book is dedicated to my wife, my travel partner in life and journey, Emily. If it were not for her patience, her dedication and her free-spirit, this book and the places in it would not have been possible. She took an ordinary girl from Vancouver and turned Ottawa into a home.

This book is also dedicated to every person I have met on the streets of Rideau, to every café and diner spot I had coffee in and every experience that has taught me a lesson and created a memory – this book goes out to you.

We travel to find ourselves, in my journey, I found the best thing in life - a home, a life.

Merylee G. Sevilla

>TOURIST

ABOUT THE AUTHOR

Merylee Sevilla originally comes from the mountainous metro hub of Vancouver, British Columbia Canada who upon graduation moved to Ottawa, Ontario for school. Within moving to Ottawa, Merylee found herself immersed in a diverse city that mixes both cultural diversity and political advocacy.

Since moving to Ottawa for school, Merylee made the official move nearly 5 years ago and has since become a local to the Ottawa area. Working as a Public Servant, she is also a published writer having written a book on coming out and one presently in the work about the Camino de Santiago. Amongst her books, Merylee often contributes to Elite Daily, Thought Catalog and a few other online magazines as a guest writer. She is pleased to have the opportunity to write for the *Greater Than a Tourist* book series.

With a passion for travel and unique experiences, Merylee found herself exploring the city she would eventually call home. From frequenting Ottawa staples like Marble Slab to visiting the luscious plains of the

Merylee G. Sevilla

Champlain Lookout – Merylee has truly become an honorary Ottawa local and hopes that others who visit will enjoy all that Ottawa has to offer.

HOW TO USE THIS BOOK

The Greater Than a Tourist book series was written by someone who has lived in an area for over three months. The goal of this book is to help travelers either dream or experience different locations by providing opinions from a local. The author has made suggestions based on their own experiences. Please do your own research before traveling to the area in case the suggested places are unavailable.

Merylee G. Sevilla

FROM THE PUBLISHER

Traveling can be one of the most important parts of a person's life. The anticipation and memories that you have are some of the best. As a publisher of the Greater Than a Tourist book series, as well as the popular 50 Things to Know book series, we strive to help you learn about new places, spark your imagination, and inspire you. Wherever you are and whatever you do I wish you safe, fun, and inspiring travel.

Lisa Rusczyk Ed. D.
CZYK Publishing

Merylee G. Sevilla

OUR STORY

Traveling is a passion of the "Greater than a Tourist" series creator. Lisa studied abroad in college, and for their honeymoon Lisa and her husband toured Europe. During her travels to Malta, an older man tried to give her some advice based on his own experience living on the island since he was a young boy. She was not sure if she should talk to the stranger but was interested in his advice. When traveling to some places she was wary to talk to locals because she was afraid that they weren't being genuine. Through her travels, Lisa learned how much locals had to share with tourists. Lisa created the "Greater Than a Tourist" book series to help connect people with locals. A topic that locals are very passionate about sharing.

Merylee G. Sevilla

>TOURIST

WELCOME TO
> TOURIST

Merylee G. Sevilla

>TOURIST

INTRODUCTION

Traveling. It leaves you speechless, then turns you into a storyteller

- Ibn Battuta

Imagine a city that is both the epicenter for political change and a cultural crockpot in one – this city exists and it is here in Ottawa, Ontario. Canada's national capital, Ottawa boasts many hidden gems that truly gives the traveler a truly unique travel experience. Whether it is a cultural experience you seek out, the flavors and cultural diversity of great food or maybe you are on the search of creating memorable memories – Ottawa has a bit of everything for everyone. The city is unique in location – surrounded by nature and water bodies, it also boasts sky rises that show a growing and metropolitan hub. Ottawa is considered the Silicon Valley of Canada. Whether you are travelling solo, with friends or family, Ottawa is the city that has it all. Visit during the winter and skate the World's longest canal come during Spring to take in the tulips

Merylee G. Sevilla

that every year are sent from Amsterdam at the Rockcliffe Pavilion – 365 days a year, Ottawa is the place to be!

>TOURIST

1. Anthony's Pizza

Imagine not having to spend thousands to go to Italy to have a unique traditional Italian pizza experience. Imagine walking through the city streets that houses local shops and businesses – where everyone seems to know everyone, here you will find Anthony's Pizza. The restaurant is set up like a small bistro with the central focus on its brick oven. With an excellent selection of wine, tiramisu paired with reasonable prices this is a great place for a date. I have even used this bistro for a romantic Valentine's Day dinner. So the next time your date wants a romantic night out or maybe they have dreams of visiting Italy – why not take them to the next best thing, Anthony's Pizza on Bank Street.

2. Champlain Lookout

Just a short walk behind the National Arts Museum lies this hidden gem of the National Capital - Champlain Lookout. There is peace and serenity that is sometimes wanted when that desire to get back to nature creeps up. The cityscape from the Lookout has been the background of many national and international photos that show the historical yet modern side of a political city that seems to be encapsulated with nature. I love to go here and watch

Merylee G. Sevilla

the sun set over the city. As darkness sets in, you can watch the lights of the city slowly flick on as the night life begins. There is nothing more local than waking early while the rest of city sleeps and take in the sunrise after having watch the sun set. Every view is unique from the last visit – making it even more magical and special.

3. Rockcliffe Pavilion

Want a spot you can truly take in the city? A spot that is unique and not crowded by tourist yet a tourist attraction? Welcome to Rockcliffe Pavilion. Rockcliffe Pavilion is a great spot for a family picnic. This place is a great way to experience nature in the heart of the city. The pavilion looks out over the Ottawa River and features a large stone gazebo. During the spring months, you can venture across the 2.65 hectare property and enjoy the bright colors and assortments of daffodils and tulips. On the premise there is a gazebo, which depending on the season you visit, is often the backdrop for many elegant and elaborate weddings. I often frequent this spot at sunrise to watch the annual hot air balloon festival in September – sometimes feeling like I myself am with them in the air. It is also a great place to take out a book and lay on the meticulously manicured lawns to read or gaze into the clouds.

>TOURIST

4. Walking Trails Behind Parliament Hill

Unknown to most tourists, there is a great walking trail in behind Parliament Hill. You can access it down by the canal lochs and Bytowne Heritage museum. I love taking this trail because it gives you a different view of the city. You get to look up at everything from below and take in the wonderment of building a city on the edge of a ravine. The trails are often frequented by local joggers and on occasion a lost tourist but sometimes getting lost behind the trails of Parliament is like being part of the history of all that takes place in the hub of Canada's policy and law making. For the political junkie, keep an eye out as the trails have been known to be a popular getaway for many Canadian politicians.

5. The Manx

There are a few restaurants in the city that one can be excused from not visiting but if there is one that no tourist or person should miss out on it is The Manx. Subtly located on Elgin Street, very few would know that this restaurant existed. You would unexpectedly walk right by. The Manx is a basement pub that boasts an out of this world breakfast menu. In the evening it is frequented by a relaxed, open minded crowd. If you are looking for a unique menu (mashed potatoes with homemade salsa for breakfast) then I highly recommend this Elgin Street pub – just because you don't miss it trying to find it.

6. Lieutenants Pump

'The Pump', as it is commonly referred to by locals, is a great pub on Elgin with a lively nightlife. With an array of craft beers to choose from this is truly a place for everyone. Boasting multiple big screen TVs showcasing the sport of the hour, take a few steps behind the bar and you'll find yourself hitting their dance floor. With local and guest DJ's 'The Pump' can get packed and busy during the summer nights especially on a Friday. When it comes to food - I highly recommend their wings. A bonus to this local stomping ground? They have a wicked breakfast menu for the post-party!

7. Pinegrove Trail

For the outdoorsy person who visits Ottawa, there are many trails to pick from; however, Pinegrove Trail is one of the National Capital Commissions (NCC) is most popular one. Imagine being able to go on a hiking trail throughout the city. I love putting on my warm clothes and trekking this trail in the winter – there is something utterly serene and beautiful about

snow covered trees and tl
one. On a hike on Pinegro
realize just how beautiful
unexpectedly stumble upo
specific place. This trail is
and is maintained year rou
nature activity. Winter or s
waiting to be explored.

8. Watson's Mill

Situated in the heritage village of Manotick, Watson's Mill has an eerie history. It is famously haunted by a ghost bride that those who visit the Mill sometimes claim they see or hear the bride. Though I have never seen her myself, I enjoy visiting the mill museum to see how flour used to be manufactured. Not to mention, if you visit during the weekend during spring and summer, you may be able to catch one of their local craft fairs where you can buy local and fresh baked goods. The staff here are usually dressed in old timey clothing and are always willing to share the chilling story of the ghost bride. If you visit during the first weekend of June you can take part in Dickinson Days, the village celebration of the town founder. If you prefer to keep to yourself – there are ample picnic tables and benches for one to have a nice meal or coffee.

A.Y. Jackson Park

out your walking shoes and go for a stroll to this quaint park in Manotick which dedicated to one of the members of the Group of Seven, A.Y. Jackson. Jackson had lived and painted in Manotick till the 60's as he was heavily influenced by the landscapes and nature found within the peaceful city. As a token of homage, A.Y. Jackson Park is topped with a rustic gazebo. This gazebo makes for the perfect spot to read a book or take in the serenity of the flowing water. The park overlooks the dam and Mill into the village. This spot is such a gem that I have considered using it as a wedding venue as nothing quite compares to nature like that of A.Y. Jackson Park.

10. Aquatopia Conservatory

If you are looking for an adventure, just travel outside the city limits just ever so slightly and you will find this beautiful modern greenhouse. From the outside, one would never know it was a greenhouse or that there could be such nature and beauty inside. Recently built this greenhouse offers a unique experience of tropical warmth combined with the feeling of being in a luscious forest of greenery. While taking in the beauty of all the growth and greenery at Aquatopia, why not stop by the café and enjoy a nice cappuccino or maybe take in a salad.

>TOURIST

This spot is a popular venue for weddings, parties and conferences. They even have a fishing pond that is fully equipped. If you are lucky during your visit, you may even get to play with their greenhouse cat that roams freely throughout the premise sometimes welcoming visitors who come far and near.

11. The Brew Pub

Located in Bell's Corners this restaurant knows how to elevate classic pub dishes – giving the pub dinner an elegant experience while mixing in the pub feel. The décor is a combination of rustic meets sophistication. The pub's unique and sophisticated atmosphere is reflected in their menu which combines everything from fish and chips, burgers and nachos along with a few unique chicken and steak platters. The staff at the pub treat customers like they are eating at 5 star restaurant but wouldn't blink an eye if you showed up wearing flannel or casually dressed in shorts and flip flops. The Brew Pub is truly the place you go to where everyone seems to know your name!

Merylee G. Sevilla

12. The Arboretum

The Arboretum is an extension of the Experimental Farm, which is located in the heart of Ottawa City. Here you can find some of the oldest and most unique trees in the city which are planted along an extensive walking path. Many of the specimens found in the Arboretum are even labelled to help wanderers explore and learn about them too. The Arboretum is a unique fixture to Ottawa as it is truly parallel to that of Central Park in New York or Stanley Park in Vancouver – all major cities who seem to find themselves within a luscious scenery of green. It truly adds a nice balance to the bustling city life.

13. The Experimental Farm

This famous farm is filled with both barn yard animals and horticultural attractions that are free to enjoy by locals and tourists alike. Take a stroll through their barns and visit popular barnyard creatures while also learning and seeing how a farm operates. For the green thumb enthusiast like myself who is more interested in plants and flowers, why not wander through the beautiful gardens to learn about the native and imported plant varieties that you could have in your very own garden. The Experimental Farm is a great place for families, with so much to see and do, it's also a great place for those who are

>TOURIST

budget conscientious yet want to have fun and learn all in one. The Experimental Farm is a travel destination that is an underrated attraction that will truly deliver in the unique Ottawa experience.

14. Hog's Back

Hog's Back is a stone throw across the street from Mooney's Bay which is a local beach in Ottawa. While many may choose the sandy beaches – Hog's Back offers a different outdoorsy feel through the hiking trails and greenery. Whether you are on foot or on a rental bike, if you follow the path you will end up at a lookout spot where you can check out the rushing rapids – perfect for any budding photographer. This hidden city gem is rarely busy and perfect for anyone looking to clear their thoughts while taking in Mother Nature and all its beauty. The rushing rapids also provides a great relaxing atmosphere, in a way making it a popular locals spot and truly a gem for visitors. Bring along your picnic basket or a good book to read as there is ample spots to take in a bite or benches to sit and read.

Merylee G. Sevilla

15. Britannia Beach

Nothing says summer is here like a day heading to the beach and unrolling the beach towel. As someone from the West Coast and who knows beaches – Britannia is a great beach to checkout in Ottawa. It is amazing that a city that is often associated for being a government and technology hub could have a place as relaxing and beautiful as Britannia. Personally, I love spending a warm summer day on the sandy beaches of Britannia, whether it is taking in the sun or simply taking in the beach activity – nothing is quite as relaxing as this. Once here, you will find that the beach offers a number of simple summer attractions and activities - from ice cream stands to help you cool down to their nice Baja Burger stand which is an outdoor bar you can order drinks and lunch while taking in the rays. Prefer something more casual and clam, why not sit back and watch kite boarders or sail boats glide by. Want to get active and moving, you can start a game of volleyball with the public nets available or take a splash in the water where you can swim or rental paddle boards and much more!

>TOURIST

16. Petrie Island

Who says you have to go down south to have an island getaway? Petrie Island is one of the most popular places for locals in Ottawa and a gem for tourists who take the opportunity to venture to the island. It is on the Ottawa River and is actually surrounded by other little islands. Equipped with public washrooms and life guards this is a great spot for a family day at the beach. Gas BBQ's are permitted here to help round out a day of outdoor fun. If you are more into learning, explore the amazing ecosystem of the island and be careful where you walk – you can find little turtles wandering around. Depending on the season, there are also opportunities to rent out kayaks and paddle boards which are a great mode of transportation and exploration on the river and the islands. The island is also a popular spot for festivities and outdoor concerts. Every summer they have their famous Cari-Vibe festival which is filled with vibrant colors from the costumes, the aroma of exotic dishes and diversity of Caribbean nations who come together to celebrate and party with both locals and tourists.

Merylee G. Sevilla

17. Planet Coffee

Are you in the mood for a caffeine kick that does not mean ordering from Starbucks or some mainstream coffee shop? Maybe you are exhausted from all that exploring but want something other than a can of Coke or bottled juice. Don't worry, go check out Planet Coffee. This local coffee shop is right in the heart of the Byward Market. Keep your eyes on the peel though, as this place is often missed by tourists and sometimes even locals because it is so well hidden down a side street, one could easily mistake it for being just a random shop or apartment. Planet Coffee offers in house baked pastries along with a great selection of coffee drinks that are made with fair-trade beans – perfect for the conscientious drinker. Want something more than coffee? They offer freshly brewed and squeezed juice as well, all of which are made in-house. Looking for something of sustenance? Don't worry – they also offer daily and freshly made sandwiches and salads. Whether you are a vegan, vegetarian or a meat eater, there is truly something for every appetite – appetizer or a full course, Planet Coffee has it all. Heads-up though, if you are thinking of stopping by- this shop is one of the only few places around that only accepts cash as payment but hitting a bank before you go is totally worth it.

>TOURIST

18. Wellington Diner

A staple in Westboro for over 50 years, the Wellington diner is always packed with patrons, as a result of this depending on when you go, you may have to wait. To a passerby, they may find it odd that there would be a slew of people waiting outside a little red suburban house – but shockingly, the Wellington Diner is actually inside this house! In a way it must be why the food that comes out of there is so good, nothing compares to a "home" cooked meal. And, if there is a place that knows food, more specifically, breakfast, it would be Wellington Diner. They do breakfast right – and it is during their mornings (especially during the weekend) that people can expect to wait for a table. What makes them the hit of most important meal? It's hard to not be a hit with their use of fresh ingredients and unique to Ottawa and the dinner dishes – depending on the sport season, they will make a dish to honor an Ottawa athlete! As a result of their fresh dishes and menus, waiting outside to get a table is well worth the wait. Not to mention that with fair prices and a laid back and relaxing atmosphere, Sunday brunches make going into Monday not so bad anymore.

19. Hip Hop Karaoke

On the third Friday of every month, wannabe artists and those looking for a night of singing head to the Elmdale Pub on Wellington. Why? Because at Elmdale they host Hip Hop Karaoke. Think you know karaoke? Don't be fooled as this isn't like any ordinary karaoke experience because there are no monitors to read the lyrics from. This is as au-natural as karaoke can get with only the background music and the participant dropping down the lyrics to their choice of song as accurately as possible. Stage fright? Can't rap? Don't worry– participants are ousted to perform rather people choose whether or not to participate. Hip Hop karaoke is always packed and a great night out if you are looking for unique night out. Plus, who knows if the night you go you hear the next Eminem, 50 Cent or Nicki Minaj dropping down the beats.

20. House Of Targ

Want a throwback to retro arcades? Well, House of Targ is as close as Ottawa gets to a retro arcade. For any tourist looking to check out this place on Bank Street, they may be confused as to where and how does one get in because House of Targ is situated between a frame shop and a boutique pet store but if you look a little closely, you will find the entrance to

House of Targ. It is essentially a basement or rather, more specifically a basement gallery of old and new school arcade games. The real highlight of this place isn't their library of games but rather their in house made perogies. They offer everything from fresh made onion and cheese perogies to varieties with a Mexican flair. Whether you go for games or perogies, House of Targ is a unique city stop for anyone looking for a throwback feel or wanting a unique experience. Visit their website or pages and see what guest performers and shows they have as on special occasions House of Targ has been known to have live performances.

21. Mayfair Theatre

Why not experience a movie just like how they use to in the 1930's? Well you can thank to The Mayfair Theatre. This theatre gives moviegoers the experience of what it was like going to a movie 'back in the day.' With only 1 large screen and extremely comfy red velvet seats, people come here to enjoy a movie the old fashioned way. The Mayfair is located on Bank Street and is considered to be one of Ottawa's oldest and active move theatres. Want a snack for the feature? Purchase some popcorn which are served in the white and red bags similar how they use to be in the old days too – which just truly adds to the genuine and unique theater experience. What kind of genre does the oldest movie theatre play? The Mayfair mostly play independent or artistic types of films making it even more of a unique outing for those who love culture and experiencing something that is completely not mainstream. Why not pay a throwback homage at the Mayfair!

22. Life Of Pie

Are you a fan of pie? Whether it is the savory or desert kind, Life of Pie is known by locals for its amazing quiches and pastries. Their menu changes weekly to showcase fresh and in season ingredients which just keep customers coming back for more. Want something more than just having a pie? Why not sign up for one of their evening activities which range from cooking classes to paint-night. Who says you can't have your pie and eat it too?

23. Marble Slab Creamery

Located in the ever so popular and quaint community of Glebe on Bank Street, Marble Slab is a custom blend ice cream shop. Where does one start? Well you begin with a base flavor of your choice followed by an array of choice of toppings to create that perfect dessert. When you have picked your toppings, the creamery masters (the person on the other side of the counter or as I say, the artist) will then combine your

>TOURIST

choice items on an ice cold marble slab to create your delicious masterpiece. I love visiting the creamery on a hot summer day and taking my masterpiece dessert on a walk through the Glebe while also visiting the local shops and boutiques.

24. Westboro Pumpkin Walk

On the evening of November 1, the carved pumpkins of Westboro Village get a second chance at life by being lit up and creating a pumpkin laneway. Whether you are a local to the area or not the folks of Westboro bring their Halloween pumpkins to a park and line the pathways with their creations. This tradition has been going on for a few years and it is a great way to keep the Halloween festivities going. In a single year, one can expect to see nearly 7000 jack o' lanterns lighting up the path. This spectacle is truly the perfect event for anyone looking to keep the spooky spirit and festivities of Halloween alive. The Westboro Pumpkin Walk is slowly growing into neighboring areas but more importantly it's a great family outing in Fall – not to mention to meet locals.

Merylee G. Sevilla

25. Flying Squirrel Trampoline Park

Did you grow up spending endless hours on the trampoline? With you could enjoy the good old days? Worried you may be too old to enjoy the trampoline? Don't worry – come to Flying Squirrel Trampoline Park and relive those glory days, or prove you aren't too old to have fun! Currently dubbed Canada's largest trampoline park, Flying Squirrel is a new addition to the city of Ottawa. Flying Squirrel Trampoline offers a variety of activities for children and adults alike. Whether you prefer to enjoy the trampoline the good old fashion way of just vertically bouncing up and down or if you enjoy a challenge and playing games, the trampoline park can help facilitate a bunch of team and group activities. They have everything from basketball, to dodge ball and bouncing around to black light and glow in the dark themes – this park has a bit of something for everyone and all bouncing levels. The Flying Squirrel is a great option for an indoor activity on those rainy or really cold days in the winter. Grab your sports gear and socks and get bouncing!

>TOURIST

26. Produce Depot

If there is one thing I miss when I travel it is the ability to cook my own meals or eat healthy. In Ottawa, there is one shop, 'The Depot' as it is affectionately called by locals, which is local Ottawa grocery store. I am a fan of Produce Depot as it offers a large array of fresh produce – they even have a butcher on hand to help find the perfect cut of meat. For the bread lovers, they have fresh baked loaves and baguettes. 'The Depot" offers products from all over the world – from Middle Eastern to Asian and Canadian – it's a shop that has diversity throughout its aisles. If you are staying in a place that allows you access to a kitchen then I recommend heading down to 'The Depot and purchasing some fresh goodness. It does not get any better than a place offering freshness, local product and unbeatable prices.

27. Ozzy's Shawarma

When you visit Ottawa, there is one thing that may stick out when you are on the hunt for a place to eat – there is a crazy large amount of shawarma restaurants in the city. Essentially for every golden arches you see, there are at least 2 to 3 shawarma places to choose from. One of those places is Ozzy's – which I must say is probably one of the greatest shawarma places in Ottawa, therefore, making it one of the most hidden gems in the city. Their chicken shawarma is deliciously moist and you can't have the sandwich without a side of their garlic potatoes to pair. I prefer their rice, as it is so perfectly seasoned, it can be a meal on its own! Ozzy's is a restaurant that is family owned and operated. This place truly is serving up amazing Lebanese food at some of the most reasonable prices you will ever find in the city. Best part about Ozzy's other than the food? You can choose to sit in and enjoy your meal in their dining area or take out and enjoy your meal at home or at a local part- either way you go, you are in for a delicious meal.

28. The Green Door

Are you vegetarian or vegan? A fan of eating organic and natural foods? The Green Door is the restaurant for you. This restaurant is located on Main Street, and has been a local staple for years. Walk in to the restaurant and you are greeted by friendly staff with many of the clienteles you see enjoying a bit are from the neighboring university. It is very low-key venue with the extravagance coming in the amazing flavors of the dishes. One would never know just by looking at the restaurant from the outside that the Green Door is a place full of flavor and unique dishes. The Green Door is a great spot for vegans, vegetarians or anyone who is having a healthy craving urge because you

>TOURIST

only pay for what you eat! The restaurant is buffet style which means you not only pick what you want to eat and try but you pay for what you consume as once you are done making your plate it is weighed and you are charged appropriately. This is the perfect setting for those who want to try a bit of everything and don't want to pay over the top prices.

29. Strathcona Park

Situated in urban Sandy Hill, a downtown neighborhood, this green space is a stretch of nature that is literally in the middle of the city. Think Central Park in Ottawa. Many local artists like to use the charming stone amphitheater to put on plays such as Shakespeare in the Park for the literature and theatre enthusiast. When there are no plays, you can walk through and imagine yourself on stage performing. For those who aren't so much a fan of the arts, you can take a stroll through the surrounding neighborhoods to see historic buildings, where many of them have been given heritage. The park also is home to the Lord Strathcona Fountain (which the park is named after) – the perfect setting for making a wish at the water fountain. Are you visiting from the US? Maldives? Russia? Italy? There is an array of embassies that surround Strathcona Park giving it the nickname of "Embassy Row", why not check in and drop by your country's home or enjoy some of the

Merylee G. Sevilla

massive and elaborate embassies that line up along the park.

30. Path Behind Canadian Museum of History

The Canadian Museum of History is just across the bridge from Ottawa and is a token hotspot for tourists as it offers one of the only IMAX theatres in the city. However, leave the grounds ever so slightly and take a stroll in behind the museum you will uncover a unique green space and the hang out spot of many locals. In a way this attraction itself is why many take the slight trip across the pond. The path behind the museum is a trail that leads to the docks and arenas of Gatineau and Ottawa – during the warmer months there are performers and festivals such as an outdoor rave and beer fest. If you are visiting during the winter months, it is one of the few places that you can enjoy a "bier" festival outdoors! More of a night owl? Why not take a walk down here to see what the city-line of Ottawa looks like. I am a fan of this view at night as it is eerily beautiful and calming especially by the water. The lights of the buildings in Ottawa give this starry illusion and with the reflection of it on the water it truly is an understatement of beauty.

>TOURIST

31. House of Georgie And Sorento's

Nothing says night cap better than a freshly made pizza from the House of Georgie and Sorento's. This literally is the place locals go to end a night of partying on a high note, not to mention ensuring you end the night on a stuffed stomach. The menu here is unique in that it offers pizza (buy a whole one or slice, depending on how hungry you are) with any imaginable topping, as well as an array of Middle Eastern dishes. Their famous pizzas are made with the freshest ingredients, not to mention the cheese and pizza sauce used are truly divine. You haven't had pizza till you have had their in-house recipes. This is going to sound crazy but the best thing on their menu in terms of a pizza flavor is the gravy pizza. That's right, you read correctly – pizza smothered in gravy, one can't say anything bad about it till they have tried it for themselves! For the foodie visiting Ottawa – you can't call yourself a foodie if you haven't tried the gravy pizza at the House of Georgie and Sorento's, don't worry if you are not as adventurous, you can stick to the traditional ones like cheese, peperoni or vegetarian!

Merylee G. Sevilla

32. Thyme And Again

Located on Wellington Street, a tourist may pass by Thyme and Again and not even realize it. Why? How? Well Thyme and Again is known as one of the best catering companies in Ottawa, but it also has a restaurant store front for those looking to experience their unique dishes. They serve fresh made gourmet meals that you can enjoy in house – they have a casually understated dining area that is warm and welcoming. If you prefer you can also take your order to go and enjoy the freshness of their dishes in the comfort of your own home. Don't expect to just leave right after your meal though – you may find yourself spending some extra time browsing through their array of unique goods for foodies.

33. Funhaven

Visiting during our colder season, or rather months? Looking for an activity that is great for families and adults alike? Look no further than Funhaven. It is exactly as it sounds – a haven for fun. Come here to play an array of traditional carnival games or take a ride in the city's only indoor roller coaster. Competitive? Why not gather some friends and play laser tag or navigate through their laser maze? Whatever it is you think is fun, Funhaven is sure to have something for you. Whether you come alone or

>TOURIST

come in a group the games at Funhaven can be played alone or with company. Plus, at the end of your visit, trade in your tickets for prizes that range from little candies to large stuffed animals and lava lamps, the perfect token and souvenir of your trip to Ottawa and Funhaven! Travel Tip – If you are in town on a Friday, come to Funhaven after 9 as they turn the place into an adult's only (19+ years old) venue where you can order a cold brew, which is perfectly served in a red solo cup and play games at the same time!

34. Princess Louise Waterfalls

One of the hidden natural gems of Ottawa is the Princess Louise Falls. The falls is located in the East side of the city and it is part of a once buried water system. Unlike many other natural wonders that require a hike and trek, these falls are fairly easy to access. The terrain is considered easy and family friendly. The falls are a spectacle making them beautiful in any season, in a way this is just one of the many reasons that makes it one of Ottawa's "must see" waterfalls in the national capital. Whether you are at the top of the falls, the bottom or somewhere in the middle, the view of the falls is unique anywhere. The Princess Louise Falls is truly a breathtaking natural beauty that is definitely an Instagram,

Facebook worthy photo op, so grab your selfie stick and visit an Ottawa must.

35. Chelsea Pub

This is an exception – while not completely in Ottawa, it is part of the National Capital Region and only a short drive across town into Quebec. The Chelsea Pub makes the list as a "must see" and visit spot. Any foodie looking for a rustic experience while enjoying burgers will truly find the Chelsea Pub the perfect place. The burgers here are unique, prepared with fresh local ingredients and served on wood cutting boards, one bite and you will want to be back for more. Not a fan of burgers? Don't worry as their menu is filled with alternatives that range from truffle macaroni and cheese to exotic appetizers. One thing is certain though when you visit the Chelsea Pub is to make sure to order a poutine on the side – there is nothing quite like a poutine from the province that made the poutine famous, Quebec.

36. The Lookout

Looking for a place where you can be you and not have to worry about being judged? Look no further than The Lookout. It is one of the best LGBTQ bars in the capital! Their licensed balcony overlooks the heart of the Byward Market making it one of the only

>TOURIST

bars in the city to have this million dollar view. The bar is found on the second level of a house like building – its' outside appeal is anything but a front of what one can expect once inside. Walk in and you will find yourself on the dance floor, go to the back of the bar and if you aren't the dancing type grab some friends and take a round of billiards. Looking for something to do during the week? Look no further than The Lookout as there is always something going on regardless of the day of the week. From their Karaoke on Mondays and Tuesdays to Ladies Night on Fridays, and then Drag Shows on Saturdays, you can rest assured there is always something entertaining and fun to see and do. With The Lookout you can expect 7 days of fun and parties, not to mention their drink specials which range from bar rail to cheekily named shots! Head to this bar if you are looking for a fun night out in town or to meet some friendly people in the LGBTQ community. Straight or gay, all is welcome to The Lookout!

37. Bad Axe Throwing

There is a craze that's going from city to city and it involves throwing axes! Though not unique to Ottawa, Bad Axe Throwing is still one of a kind. Put on your lucky plaid shirt and visit Bad Axe Throwing, where the staff are friendly and knowledgeable. They will give you the tips and tricks on to throw and axe and for those newbies, they will teach you how to launch an axe at a wooden bull's eye. Have a party? Or part of a large group? No worries, as you are allowed to bring your own beer and food to make it an even better personal experience. They offer walk-in time slots but just to be safe, visit them online or on their various social media platforms to book a time slot or to see if they have any special deals and offers. Looking to stay in town longer? They offer leagues where you can compete and win a special medal!

38. Burgers And Shakes

Travelling and craving a juicy burger? Maybe you are on the hunt for the best burger? Look no further than this family owned and operated spot, Burgers and Shakes. It has been a staple in the Ottawa South area for over 2 decades. They offer a large variety of burgers (meat, vegetarian or fish) made to order along with a side of fries or onion rings. To complement their freshly grilled burgers and fresh cut fries, their milkshakes are unlike any other you will ever try. There are a handful of flavors to choose from, from coffee to strawberry and a combination of flavors too. There is a reason they are called "Burgers And Shakes" and it's because their burgers and shakes are truly the talk of town. After a bite or maybe beforehand, why not take in a round of golf at their driving range or mini putt that are just a step away. Don't worry if you forget your clubs, you can rent them for 2 dollars and a 100 rounds of balls are only ten dollars – making this a cost-friendly excursion.

39. Jaymes White Show

Do you believe in the art of mindreading? Are you a skeptic? If you are lucky enough to be in town during a time that has a Jaymes White performance, I highly recommended grabbing a pair of tickets. White is a local entertainer and acclaimed mentalist and was even awarded Entertainer of the Year in Ottawa. He has the ability to know what you are thinking as well as perform mind blowing illusions that will leave you wondering – how did he do that? Spend an evening at a local venue (usually a bar, theatre or museum) and experience a once in a lifetime interactive illusionist show. If you are visiting during the months of September to October, check out his séance performances at various haunted places throughout the city. It is a truly spine thrilling experience that will leave you shaking and mind blown and asking, "how'd he do it?".

Merylee G. Sevilla

40. The Loft

A fan of board games? Looking for something low key? Want a place that combines drinking with Monopoly? Look no further than Loft, it is the place to be for anyone looking for a "stay in activity". The Loft is a great place for an alternative night out or rather night in. Known as a 'board game café' it is a totally different way to spend some time in the city mingling with locals. Once you arrive, you will pay a small fee (typically $5 and it helps maintain their collections) and then you choose where you would like to be seated. Once inside and seated, you will see the walls of the venue are lined with board games both new and old, books and mind puzzles – not to mention, they offer a fully stocked bar both with alcoholic and non-nonalcoholic. What better recipe for fun and laughter than board games and booze. Depending on the night, there may be themed drinks – everything from Harry Potter to Game of Thrones, this unique spot in Ottawa is the fun-haven for board game lovers.

41. Saunders Farm

Saunders Farm is another Ottawa outdoors activity. The farm rests on 100-acres of land and is locally famous for its haunted hayride that is sure to get any visitor screaming and oozing with fear. Don't be

>TOURIST

scared off though as Saunders Farm has a ton to offer when it comes to entertainment value. In a way this is what makes the farm a popular tourist hot-spot all year round, whether it is in the fall or summer months one comes. For the farm specifically, there is a huge influx of visitors that come in the month of October. They are known for giving the both locals and visitors of Ottawa a mighty great scare. If you are not a fan of having your pants scared off- don't worry there is still plenty for you to do! There are corn mazes, splash pads for those who come in the summer months and want to cool down. For the city folks looking to experience farm and country life, hop on for a hayride – the perfect activity for those looking for a tamer experience. Their mazes have actually earned Saunders Farm the reputation for having the largest collection of full-sized hedge mazes in North America.

42. Park Omega

Imagine being up close and personal with some of nature is wildest and rarest animals? Check out Park Omega, which is a zoo that allows you to drive through various animals habitats, not to mention, get the opportunity to get close enough so you can feed some of the animals too. The park spans over 12 km and has a park trail which takes about 1.5 hours to drive through. As you drive through, you can see animals such as reindeers, bison and elk all of which will come right up to your car to get close and personal with you. Want to take the experience to the next level? There are trails and zones where you can walk up and pet some of the animals but also take in some of the educational and unique shows such as Birds of Prey, where you can learn about different types of predatory birds. Stop by their lake and ponds and purchase some pellets to attract some of the water creatures they have. Open all year round, rain, snow or sunshine – Park Omega is a unique and fun experience for all.

43. The Maze - Maple Hill Urban Farm

Each summer Maple Hill Farms grows a serious corn maze that will have visitors trying to figure their way out. The elaborate mazes will definitely require one to use your senses and brain smarts to navigate the web. Brain smart? Why not test your Canadian history knowledge with their trivia challenge that makes the experience of getting out of their elaborate mazes that much more difficult. Imagine an escape room but in a life sized 10 acre labyrinth. Up for the challenge? Visiting in the fall months? Why not stop by and hop on aboard the tractor and take a ride through their pumpkin patch. Once in the pumpkin path – feeling a bit creative? Or feeling inspired? Walk through the

>TOURIST

patch and find the perfect pumpkin to carve and showcase your carving skills during Halloween! The farm also offers more than just activities, they offer a local product market selling only local grown and harvested products. They also have an Alpaca farm which – if you haven't done this yet, it is HIGHLY recommended. Who wouldn't enjoy walking with an Alpaca?

44. Karter's Korner

Have a need for speed? Karter's Korner is go-karting at its finest! A local hot spot for those who enjoy a fast thrill. Why not grab a group of friends (kids welcome) and get your need for speed fix. The outdoor track is designed for drivers of all levels and is lined with rubber tires to ensure safety for all. Looking for another form of adrenaline rush? Karter's Korner also offers paintball outdoors and mini golf for those looking for a more low-key activity. Whether it's a thrill or a family-friendly activity, Karter's Korner is a one-stop of family fun.

Merylee G. Sevilla

45. Rideau Carleton Horse Racing

Operating all year round, the Rideau Carleton Raceway boasts a unique style of entertainment – horse racing. Professional drivers are pulled in buggies by horses around the race track. Looking to see how lucky you are? Why not make a bet to see if you can win big. Not the gambling type? Why not order up a drink and snacks and take in the show from the comfortable spectators' view which allow you to take in the races either inside or out. Local insider tip - their breakfast buffet is one of the best in the city, so why not take in a race while enjoying the best buffet in town.

46. Elgin Street Diner

After a night of dancing and exploring the city, what better way to keep the night going than visiting Elgin Street Diner? Located on Elgin Street, this diner has been around for over two decades and has won an array of accolades – one such praise is being Ottawa's Best Diner! Visiting Elgin Street Diner after a night on the town will be doing yourself a huge favor as their menu has something for everyone and their cravings whether its greasy or not. Notoriously famous for their poutine and milkshakes, no matter

>TOURIST

how late or early it is, Elgin Street Diner is open 24/7. Don't think you can make to the restaurant? Don't worry, the Diner is also part of Skip the Dishes a delivery application that can fix your cravings with the simple push of a button. So if you are looking for a night in with room service, order up some diner food and enjoy Ottawa from the comforts of your hotel bed.

47. Ottawa Fury Game

GOAL! Are you a soccer (or football as some call it) fan? Why not check out the local soccer team, Ottawa Fury and enjoy what will truly be an evening of exciting field action and family entertainment. Ticket game prices are very reasonable (as low as $15/ticket). The Ottawa Fury play at the newly built and designed TD Place Stadium in Lansdowne Park – which is in the heart of the city and surrounded by restaurants and local boutique shops. Grabbing a bite before the game? Don't worry because the stadium is within walking distances of an assortment of restaurants that range from a savory and sweet crepe restaurant to a modern pizzeria, there is literally everything one could crave before a game! While at the game, why not take your picture with Sparky the mascot or stick around after the game to get players signatures to forever commemorate your experience at Canada's capital soccer team, the Ottawa Fury.

Merylee G. Sevilla

What better way to get up close and personal with some of Ottawa's and Canada's athletes.

48. Ottawa's Christmas Light Show

For the traveler visiting during the winter months two pieces of advice: one, bring a warm puffy coat and two, Ottawa's Christmas Light Show. This is a winter holiday must see and do activity. Every December Ottawa puts on the greatest light show in the city. Located in Corkstown Road, the path is transformed into a Christmas light display that runs synchronized to Christmas music classics. The best part? You don't have to worry about the cold temperatures or get tired walking because the Ottawa Christmas Lights Show is experienced from the comfort of your car. Once you enter the premise you will be driving through a 2 km stretch of lights and song. What better way to enjoy the holiday spirit while traveling than with friends and family. This activity is best enjoyed while sipping on some hot chocolate topped with marshmallows. An added bonus to this activity? A portion of the proceeds of the light show go towards local charities in the city!

>TOURIST

49. Stoneface Dolly's

Any foodie visiting Ottawa can't come to Ottawa without visiting Stoneface Dolly's. Located on Preston Street (which is in the heart of Ottawa's Italian community) but this inconspicuous diner looks like, well any ordinary place however Stoneface Dolly's is so much more than "ordinary". Stoneface Dolly's is actually a popular and favorite "it" spot for Ottawa locals. The chefs here use an array of global inspirations to create unique meals such as the bobite and jerk ribs. Looking for something more traditional? Don't worry they offer burgers and fries and steaks for the more traditional folks. Just a glimpse at their menu and you will see that this deceivingly subtle restaurant has so much to offer. Looking for a brunch spot? Better get in line early as they offer brunch that is not only legendary but an experience worth trying at least once. Not to mention, coming to Stoneface Dolly's is easy on the bank account which makes the experience that much more enjoyable!

Merylee G. Sevilla

50. Valleyview Farm

Take a trip to the west side of the city to visit this outdoor petting farm. At Valleyview, kids and adults can learn about the amount of work that it takes to operate a farm while also spending time with their barnyard animals. Valleyview Farm, depending on the season will host an array of events like an Easter Egg Hunt which is great fun for everyone in the family. While the farm is typically geared towards children, it is just as much fun for adults. There is a mini train that one pays a small fee to take a tour of the premises – think of it as a laid-back approach to exploring Valleyview. This little farm is a great place to take a city-slicker and put them to work experiencing this unique farm and country life. It will definitely give a different perspective and insight!

>TOURIST

TOP REASONS TO BOOK THIS TRIP

When it comes to Ottawa, don't waste a minute hesitating whether or not you should come to Canada's capital. You won't be disappointed as you will truly enjoy everything this city has to offer.

From the peaceful serenity of green space mixed with metropolitan all in one. The food which represents the truly diverse communities and cultures in the heart of the nation's capital.

And finally, the exposure of culture and history to which at every step and turn you will feel as if you were there as it all unfolded. What better reason to visit Ottawa than the fact that you can enjoy everything from shopping to museums and to nature and beaches – this is a city that has so much to offer for those on an expedition!

Merylee G. Sevilla

Bonus Book

50 THINGS TO KNOW ABOUT PACKING LIGHT FOR TRAVEL

Pack the Right Way Every Time

Author: Manidipa Bhattacharyya

Merylee G. Sevilla

First Published in 2015 by Dr. Lisa Rusczyk. Copyright 2015. All Rights Reserved. No part of this publication may be reproduced, including scanning and photocopying, or distributed in any form or by any means, electronic or mechanical, or stored in a database or retrieval system without prior written permission from the publisher.

Disclaimer: The publisher has put forth an effort in preparing and arranging this book. The information provided herein by the author is provided "as is". Use this information at your own risk. The publisher is not a licensed doctor. Consult your doctor before engaging in any medical activities. The publisher and author disclaim any liabilities for any loss of profit or commercial or personal damages resulting from the information contained in this book.

Edited by Melanie Howthorne

Introduction

He who would travel happily
must travel light.

-Antoine de Saint-Exupéry

Travel takes you to different places from seas and mountains to deserts and much more. In your travels you get to interact with different people and their cultures. You will, however, enjoy the sights and interact positively with these new people even more, if you are travelling light.

When you travel light your mind can be free from worry about your belongings. You do not have to spend precious vacation time waiting for your luggage to arrive after a long flight. There is be no chance of your bags going missing and the best part is that you need not pay a fee for checked baggage.

People who have mastered this art of packing light will root for you to take only one carry-on, wherever you go. However, many people can find it really hard to pack light. More so if you are travelling with children. Differentiating between "must have" and "just in case" items is the starting point. There will be ample shopping avenues at your destination which are just waiting to be explored.

Merylee G. Sevilla

This book will show you 'packing' in a new 'light' – pun intended – and help you to embrace light packing practices for all of your future travels.

Off to packing!

Dedication

I dedicate this book to all the travel buffs that I know, who have given me great insights into the contents of their backpacks.

About The Author

Manidipa Bhattacharyya is a creative writer and editor, with an education in English literature and Linguistics. After working in the IT industry for seven long years she decided to call it quits and follow her heart instead. Manidipa has been ghost writing, editing, proof reading and doing secondary research services for many story tellers and article writers for about three years. She stays in Kolkata, India with her husband and a busy two year old. In her own time Manidipa enjoys travelling, photography and writing flash fiction.

Manidipa believes in travelling light and never carries anything that she couldn't haul herself on a trip. However, travelling with her child changed the scenario. She seemed to carry the entire world with her for the baby on the first two trips. But good sense prevailed and she is again working her way to becoming a light traveler, this time with a kid.

Merylee G. Sevilla

The Right Travel Gear
1. Choose Your Travel Gear Carefully

While selecting your travel gear, pick items that are light weight, durable and most importantly, easy to carry. There are cases with wheels so you can drag them along – these are usually on the heavy side because of the trolley. Alternatively a backpack that you can carry comfortably on your back, or even a duffel bag that you can carry easily by hand or sling across your body are also great options. Whatever you choose, one thing to keep in mind is that the luggage itself should not weigh a ton, this will give you the flexibility to bring along one extra pair of shoes if you so desire.

2. Carry The Minimum Number Of Bags

Selecting light weight luggage is not everything. You need to restrict the number of bags you carry as well. One carry-on size bag is ideal for light travel. Most carriers allow one cabin baggage plus one purse, handbag or camera bag as long as it slides under the seat in front. So technically, you can carry two items of luggage without checking them in.

Merylee G. Sevilla

3. Pack One Extra Bag

Always pack one extra empty bag along with your essential items. This could be a very light weight duffel bag or even a sturdy tote bag which takes up minimal space. In the event that you end up buying a lot of souvenirs, you already have a handy bag to stuff all that into and do not have to spend time hunting for an appropriate bag.

> *I'm very strict with my packing and have everything in its right place. I never change a rule. I hardly use anything in the hotel room. I wheel my own wardrobe in and that's it.*
>
> Charlie Watts

Clothes & Accessories
4. Plan Ahead

Figure out in advance what you plan to do on your trip. That will help you to pick that one dress you need for the occasion. If you are going to attend a wedding then you have to carry formal wear. If not, you can ditch the gown for something lighter that will be comfortable during long walks or on the beach.

5. Wear That Jacket

Remember that wearing items will not add extra luggage for your air travel. So wear that bulky jacket that you plan to carry for your trip. This saves space and can also help keep you warm during the chilly flight.

6. Mix and Match

Carry clothes that can be interchangeably used to reinvent your look. Find one top that goes well with a couple of pairs of pants or skirts. Use tops, shirts and jackets wisely along with other accessories like a scarf or a stole to create a new look.

7. Choose Your Fabric Wisely

Stuffing clothes in cramped bags definitely takes its toll which results in wrinkles. It is best to carry wrinkle free, synthetic clothes or merino tops. This will eliminate the need for that small iron you usually bring along.

8. Ditch Clothes Pack Underwear

Pack more underwear and socks. These are the things that will give you a fresh feel even if you do not get a chance to wear fresh clothes. Moreover these are easy to wash and can be dried inside the hotel room itself.

9. Choose Dark Over Light

While picking your clothes choose dark coloured ones. They are easy to colour coordinate and can last longer before needing a wash. Accidental food spills and dirt from the road are less visible on darker clothes.

10. Wear Your Jeans

Take only one pair of Jeans with you, which you should wear on the flight. Remember to pick a pair that can be worn for sightseeing trips and is equally eloquent for dinner. You can add variety by adding light weight cargoes and chinos.

11. Carry Smart Accessories

The right accessory can give you a fresh look even with the same old dress. An intelligent neck-piece, a couple of bright scarves, stoles or a sarong can be used in a number of ways to add variety to your clothing. These light weight beauties can double up as a nursing cover, a light blanket, beach wear, a modesty cover for visiting places of worship, and also makes for an enthralling game of peek-a-boo.

\>TOURIST

12. Learn To Fold Your Garments

Seasoned travellers all swear by rolling their clothes for compact and wrinkle free packing. Bundle packing, where you roll the clothes around a central object as if tying it up, is also a popular method of compact and wrinkle free packing. Stacking folded clothes one on top of another is a big no-no as it makes creases extreme and they are difficult to get rid of without ironing.

13. Wash Your Dirty Laundry

One of the ways to avoid carrying loads of clothes is to wash the clothes you carry. At some places you might get to use the laundry services or a Laundromat but if you are in a pinch, best solution is to wash them yourself. If that is the plan then carrying quick drying clothes is highly recommended, which most often also happen to be the wrinkle free variety.

14. Leave Those Towels Behind

Regular towels take up a lot of space, are heavy and take ages to dry out. If you are staying at hotels they will provide you with towels anyway. If you are travelling to a remote place, where the availability of towels look doubtful, carry a light weight travel towel of viscose material to do the job.

15. Use A Compression Bag

Compression bags are getting lots of recommendation now days from regular travellers. These are useful for saving space in your luggage when you have to pack bulky dresses. While packing for the return trip, get help from the hotel staff to arrange a vacuum cleaner.

Footwear

16. Put On Your Hiking Boots

If you have plans to go hiking or trekking during your trip, you will need those bulky hiking boots. The best way to carry them is to wear them on flight to save space and luggage weight. You can remove the boots once inside and be comfortable in your socks.

17. Picking The Right Shoes

Shoes are often the bulkiest items, along with being the dainty if you are a female. They need care and take up a lot of space in your luggage. It is advisable therefore to pick shoes very carefully. If you plan to do a lot of walking and site seeing, then wearing a pair of comfortable walking shoes are a must. For more formal occasions you can carry durable, light weight flats which will not take up much space.

> TOURIST

18. Stuff Shoes

If you happen to pack a pair of shoes, ensure you utilize their hollow insides. Tuck small items like rolled up socks or belts to save space. They will also be easy to find.

Toiletries
19. Stashing Toiletries

Carry only absolute necessities. Airline rules dictate that for one carry-on bag, liquids and gels must be in 3.4 ounce (100ml) bottles or less, and must be packed in a one quart zip-lock bag. If you are planning to stay in a hotel, the basic things will be provided for you. It's best is to buy the rest from the local market at your destination.

20. Take Along Tampons

Tampons are a hard to find item in a lot of countries. Figure out how many you need and pack accordingly. For longer stays you can buy them online and have them delivered to where you are staying.

21. Get Pampered Before You Travel

Some avid travellers suggest getting a pedicure and manicure just the day before travelling. This not only gives you a well kept look, you also save the trouble of packing nail polish. Remember, every little bit of weight reduced adds up.

Electronics
22. Lugging Along Electronics

Electronics have a large role to play in our lives today. Most of us cannot imagine our lives away from our phones, laptops or tablets. However while travelling, one must consider the amount of weight these electronics add to our luggage. Thankfully smart phones come along with all the essentials tools like a camera, email access, picture editing tools and more. They are smart to the point of eliminating the need to carry multiple gadgets. Choose a smart phone that suits all your requirements and travel with the world in your palms or pocket.

23. Reduce the Number of Chargers

If you do travel with multiple electronic devices, you will have to bear the additional burden of carrying all their chargers too. Check if a single charger can be used for multiple devices. You might also consider investing in a pocket charger. These small devices support multiple devices while keeping you charged on the go.

>TOURIST

24. Travel Friendly Apps

Along with smart phones come numerous apps, which are immensely helpful in our travels. You name it and you have an app for it at hand – take pictures, sharing with friends and family, torch to light dark roads, maps, checking flight/train times, find hotels and many other things. Use these smart alternatives to traditional items like books to eliminate weight and save space.

I get ideas about what's essential when packing my suitcase.

-Diane von Furstenberg

Travelling With Kids
25. Bring Along the Stroller

Kids might enjoy walking for a while but they soon tire out and a stroller is the just the right thing for them to rest in while you continue your tour. Strollers also double duty as a luggage carrier and shopping bag holder. Remember to pick a light weight, easy to handle brand of stroller. Better yet, find out in advance if you can rent a stroller at your destination.

26. Bring Only Enough Diapers for Your Trip

Diapers take up a lot of space and add to the weight of your luggage. Therefore it is advisable to carry just enough diapers to last through the trip and a few for afterwards, till you buy fresh stock at your destination. Unless of course you are travelling to a really remote area, in which case you have no choice but to carry the load. Otherwise diapers are something you will find pretty easily.

27. Take Only A Couple Of Toys

Children are easily attracted by new things in their environment. While travelling they will find numerous 'new' objects to scrutinize and play with. Packing just one favorite toy is enough, or if there is no favorite toy leave out all of them in favor of stories or imaginary games.

28. Carry Kid Friendly Snacks

Create a small snack counter in your bag to store away quick bites for those sudden hunger pangs. Depending on the child's age this could include chocolates, raisins, dry fruits, granola bars or biscuits. Also keep a bottle of water handy for your little one. These things do not add much weight and can be adjusted in a handbag or knapsack.

>TOURIST

29. Games to Carry

Create some travel specific, imaginary games if you have slightly grown up children, like spot the attractions. Keep a coloring book and colors handy for in-flight or hotel time. Apps on your smart phone can keep the children engaged with cartoons and story books. Older children are often entertained by games available on phones or tablets. This cuts the weight of luggage down while keeping the kids entertained.

30. Let the Kids Carry Their Load

A good thing is to start early sharing of responsibilities. Let your child pick a bag of his or her choice and pack it themselves. Keep tabs on what they are stuffing in their bags by asking if they will be using that item on the trip. It could start out being just an entertainment bag initially but with growing years they will learn to sort the useful from the superfluous. Children as little as four can maneuver a small trolley suitcase like a pro- their experience in pull along toys credit. If you are worried that you may be pulling it for them, you may want to start with a backpack.

31. Decide on Location for Children to Sleep

While on a trip you might not always get a crib at your destination, and carrying one will make life all the more difficult. Instead call ahead to see if there are any cribs or roll out beds for children. You may even put blankets on the floor. Weave them a story about camping and they will gladly sleep without any trouble.

32. Get Baby Products Delivered At Your Destination

If you are absolutely paranoid about not getting your favourite variety of diaper or brand of baby food, check out online stores like amazon.com for services in your destination city. You can buy things online ahead of your travel and get them delivered to your hotel upon arrival.

33. Feeding Needs Of Your Infants

If you are travelling with a breastfed infant, you save the trouble of carrying bottles and bottle sanitization kits. For special food, or medications, you may need to call ahead to make sure you have a refrigerator where you are staying.

34. Feeding Needs of Your Toddler

With the progression from infancy to toddler, their dietary requirements too evolve. You will have to pack some snacks for travelling time. Fresh fruits and

>TOURIST

vegetables can be purchased at your destination. Most of the cities you travel to in whichever part of the world, will have baby food products and formulas, available at the local drug-store or the supermarket.

35. Picking Clothes for Your Baby

Contrary to popular belief, babies can do without many changes of clothes. At the most pack 2 outfits per day. Pack mix and match type clothes for your little one as well. Pick things which are comfortable to wear and quick to dry.

36. Selecting Shoes for Your Baby

Like outfits, kids can make do with two pairs of comfortable shoes. If you can get some water resistant shoes it will be best. To expedite drying wet shoes, you can stuff newspaper in them then wrap them with newspaper and leave them to dry overnight.

37. Keep One Change of Clothes Handy

Travelling with kids can be tricky. Keep a change of clothes for the kids and mum handy in your purse or tote bag. This takes a bit of space in your hand luggage but comes extremely handy in case there are any accidents or spills.

38. Leave Behind Baby Accessories

Baby accessories like their bed, bath tub, car seat, crib etc. should be left at home. Many hotels provide a crib on request, while car seats can be borrowed from friends or rented. Babies can be given a bath in the hotel sink or even in the adult bath tub with a little bit of water. If you bring a few bath toys, they can be used in the bath, pool, and out of water. They can also be sanitized easily in the sink.

39. Carry a Small Load Of Plastic Bags

With children around there are chances of a number of soiled clothes and diapers. These plastic bags help to sort the dirt from the clean inside your big bag. These are very light weight and come in handy to other carry stuff as well at times.

Pack with a Purpose
40. Packing for Business Trips

One neutral-colored suit should suffice. It can be paired with different shirts, ties and accessories for different occasions. One pair of black suit pants could be worn with a matching jacket for the office or with a snazzy top for dinner.

41. Packing for A Cruise

Most cruises have formal dinners, and that formal dress usually takes up a lot of space. However you might find a tuxedo to rent. For women, a short black dress with multiple accessory options will do the trick.

42. Packing for A Long Trip Over Different Climates

The secret packing mantra for travel over multiple climates is layering. Layering traps air around your body creating insulation against the cold. The same light t-shirt that is comfortable in a warmer climate can be the innermost layer in a colder climate.

Reduce Some More Weight
43. Leave Precious Things At Home

Things that you would hate to lose or get damaged leave them at home. Precious jewelry, expensive gadgets or dresses, could be anything. You will not require these on your trip. Leave them at home and spare the load on your mind.

44. Send the Load Of Souvenirs By Post

If you have spent all your money on purchasing souvenirs, carrying them back in the same bag that you brought along would be difficult. Either pack everything in another bag and check it in the airport or get everything shipped to your home. Use an international carrier for a secure transit, but this could be more expensive than the checking fees at the airport.

45. Avoid Carrying Books

Books equal to weight. There are many reading apps which you can download on your smart phone or tab. Plus there are gadgets like Kindle and Nook that are thinner and lighter alternatives to your regular book.

Check, Get, Set, Check Again
46. Strategize Before Packing

Create a travel list and prepare all that you think you need to carry along. Keep everything on your bed or floor before packing and then think through once again – do I really need that? Any item that meets this question can be avoided. Remove whatever you don't really need and pack the rest.

47. Test Your Luggage

Once you have fully packed for the trip take a test trip with your luggage. Take your bags and go to town for window shopping for an hour. If you enjoy your hour long trip it is good to go, if not, go home and reduce the load some more. Repeat this test till you hit the right weight.

48. Add a Roll Of Duct Tape

You might wonder why, when this book has been talking about reducing stuff, we're suddenly asking you to pack something totally unusual. This is because when you have limited supplies, duct tape is immensely helpful for small repairs – a broken bag, leaking zip-lock bag, broken sunglasses, you name it and duct tape can fix it, temporarily.

49. Our List of Essential Items

Even though the emphasis is on packing light, there are things which have to be carried for any trip. Here is our list of essentials:

- Passport/Visa or any other ID
- Any other paper work that might be required on a trip like permits, hotel reservation confirmations etc.

- Medicines – all your prescription medicines and emergency kit, especially if you are travelling with children

- Medical or vaccination records

- Money in foreign currency if travelling to a different country

- Tickets- Email or Message them to your phone

50. Make the Most Of Your Trip

Wherever you are going, whatever you hope to do we encourage you to embrace it whole-heartedly. Take in the scenery, the culture and above all, enjoy your time away from home.

On a long journey even a straw weighs heavy.

-Spanish Proverb

\>TOURIST

Read other Greater Than a Tourist Books

Greater Than a Tourist San Miguel de Allende Guanajuato Mexico: 50 Travel Tips from a Local by Tom Peterson

Greater Than a Tourist – Lake George Area New York USA: 50 Travel Tips from a Local by Janine Hirschklau

Greater Than a Tourist – Monterey California United States: 50 Travel Tips from a Local by Katie Begley

Greater Than a Tourist – Chanai Crete Greece: 50 Travel Tips from a Local by Dimitra Papagrigoraki

Greater Than a Tourist – The Garden Route Western Cape Province South Africa: 50 Travel Tips from a Local by Li-Anne McGregor van Aardt

Greater Than a Tourist – Sevilla Andalusia Spain: 50 Travel Tips from a Local by Gabi Gazon

Greater Than a Tourist – Kota Bharu Kelantan Malaysia: 50 Travel Tips from a Local by Aditi Shukla

Children's Book: Charlie the Cavalier Travels the World by Lisa Rusczyk

Merylee G. Sevilla

> TOURIST GREATER THAN A TOURIST

Visit GreaterThanATourist.com:
http://GreaterThanATourist.com

Sign up for the Greater Than a Tourist Newsletter:
http://eepurl.com/cxspyf

Follow us on Facebook:
https://www.facebook.com/GreaterThanATourist

Follow us on Pinterest:
http://pinterest.com/GreaterThanATourist

Follow us on Instagram:
http://Instagram.com/GreaterThanATourist

Follow on Twitter:
http://twitter.com/ThanaTourist

Merylee G. Sevilla

> TOURIST GREATER THAN A TOURIST

Please leave your honest review of this book on Amazon and Goodreads. Thank you. We appreciate your positive and constructive feedback. Thank you.

Merylee G. Sevilla

>TOURIST

NOTES

Made in the USA
Middletown, DE
10 October 2021